Portrait of the
PACIFIC RIM

Ole Hoyer and
Wendy Snowdon

HERITAGE

VICTORIA | VANCOUVER | CALGARY

Heritage House Publishing Company Ltd.
heritagehouse.ca

LIBRARY AND ARCHIVES CANADA CATALOGUING IN PUBLICATION
Hoyer, Ole
Portrait of the Pacific Rim / Ole Hoyer and Wendy Snowdon.

ISBN 978-1-927051-32-0

1. Pacific Rim National Park Reserve (B.C.)—Pictorial works.
2. Tofino (B.C.)—Pictorial works. I. Snowdon, Wendy II. Title.

FC3844.4.H69 2012   971.1'2   C2011-908230-6

Edited by Kate Scallion
Proofread by Karla Decker
Cover and book design by Jacqui Thomas
Cover photos: Aerial view of Chesterman beach (front); starfish and
anemones, northwest view from the Wild Pacific Trail near Ucluelet (back)
Title page: Aerial view of Long Beach, Pacific Rim National Park Reserve
Copyright page: Old-growth forest along the Rainforest Trail

This book was produced using FSC-certified, acid-free paper,
processed chlorine free and printed with vegetable-based inks.

Heritage House acknowledges the financial support for its publishing program
from the Government of Canada through the Canada Book Fund (CBF),
Canada Council for the Arts and the province of British Columbia through
the British Columbia Arts Council and the Book Publishing Tax Credit.

16 15 14 13 12   1 2 3 4 5

Printed in Canada

PACIFIC RIM

top A dead Sitka spruce against a cobalt blue sky is an arresting sight. These trees are the tallest conifers in North America and can live to be 800 years old.

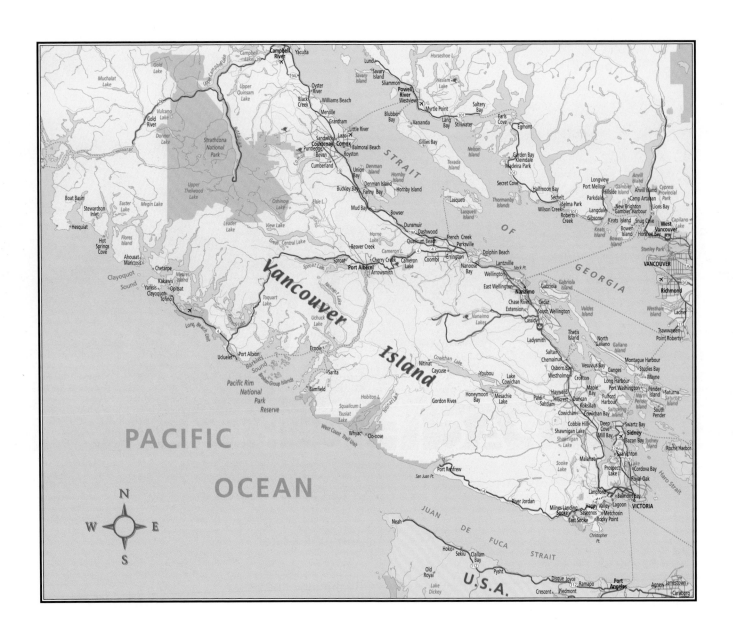

THE PACIFIC RIM

A visit to Pacific Rim National Park Reserve is an unforgettable experience. In only a few hours of travelling on Highway 4 from the eastern side of Vancouver Island, you will feel as though you've covered a great distance through the wilderness, and upon arriving at the far end of the Island, you have in fact reached the very western edge of Canada. Beyond, the mighty Pacific Ocean stretches, with few interruptions, for thousands of kilometres.

From Parksville to Coombs, Cathedral Grove to Port Alberni, the drive to the coast is a memorable part of the Pacific Rim experience. The quaint market in Coombs, with goats on the roof, and the towering, centuries-old trees of Cathedral Grove are essential places to stop and take in what lies at the doorstep of the Pacific Rim. The twisting route winds its way through snatches of rainforest over mountains and ends where the Pacific Ocean laps the western shore of Vancouver Island.

It is this combination of land and sea that makes Pacific Rim such a compelling destination. Its huge beaches and primordial rainforests form an ecosystem unlike anything else in the world. It's a place to learn about and experience the power and beauty of nature.

Pacific Rim National Park Reserve is made up of three units: Long Beach, which lies between the villages of Tofino and Ucluelet; the Broken Group Islands, which is a haven for paddlers; and the West Coast Trail, which is renowned worldwide as a challenging, gorgeous multiday hike. This book features the beaches, mountains and forests of Long Beach and Clayoquot Sound, the Broken Group Islands Unit, the K^wisitis Visitor Centre, as well as the villages of Tofino and Ucluelet.

Long before the area became known to modern-day travellers, it was home to the First Nations people known as the Nuu-chah-nulth (pronounced "Noo-CHA-noolth"). For thousands of years, these people of the coast and the mountains benefited from the abundance of the sea. They are still very much at home here, and their spirits infuse the area, though their lifestyle has changed as settlers have arrived.

Visitors come here to enjoy a wealth of outdoor activities, including hiking, camping, surfing, fishing and sea kayaking. The busy season is summer, when almost every accommodation, from the simplest campsite to the most luxurious hotel room, is full every night.

Winter, when raging storms roar in from the Pacific, is also popular time to visit. Adventure-seeking visitors come to watch the huge waves from the safety of upscale

top Bald eagles are a common sight in Pacific Rim. The majestic birds, which are expert fishers, can attain a wingspan of 2.5 metres. The Barkley Sound area near Ucluelet has one of the highest concentrations of bald eagles in the world.

beachfront inns and, when the storms have cleared, they enjoy solitude and beauty on the grandest scale.

However, even in the busy season there is never a crowded feeling in Pacific Rim. The beaches are wide, sandy and long, offering plenty of space for everyone who comes to explore, wade, sunbathe or walk. Beginning just outside Tofino—which is perched at the tip of the Esowista Peninsula—beaches stretch along Wickaninnish Bay and Florencia Bay for dozens of kilometres. The most famous is Long Beach, made up of a string of named and nameless beaches, coves and inlets. Energetic hikers can walk Long Beach from Schooner Cove in the north to Halfmoon Bay at the far end, some 20 kilometres to the south.

The beach is bordered by a magnificently thick, old-growth rainforest. Numerous trails and boardwalks wind through the woods, allowing visitors to see and learn about the enormous primeval trees that live there and about their cycle of life.

Next door to Pacific Rim is Clayoquot (pronounced KLA-kwut or CLAY-oh-kwut) Sound, a UNESCO Biosphere Reserve. These coastal waters are rich in a great variety of aquatic life, from colourful starfish to immense gray whales. The islands in the Sound are filled with stands of thousand-year-old trees and are home to the Nuu-chah-nulth people.

People are drawn to the area because of the water. Venturing into the waters of Tofino Inlet or Clayoquot Sound in a sea kayak, traditional cedar canoe or sightseeing motorboat, visitors experience one of the most pristine environments in the world. Surfers and paddle surfers play in the breakers along the beaches, sometime sharing the water with seals and sea lions who share their love of the waves. Whale-watching trips allow visitors to approach majestic gray whales, while those on fishing charters return home with fresh trophy salmon or halibut.

In these pages, Pacific Rim is captured at its best: in sunny summers, on misty mornings, among ancient trees, with the ocean never far away. Enjoy the images as a reminder of your visit . . . and as an invitation to return again soon.

GOING COASTAL

opposite With the aid of the spring run-off, the Upper Falls at Little Qualicum Falls Provincial Park turn into a torrent of water cascading deep into the canyon below.

top Coombs is best known for its famous "Goats on the Roof" Old Country Market, shop and restaurant, a favourite stopover for both locals and tourists on their way to the coast.

There are few experiences that truly embody the cliché about the journey being just as important as the destination as does the drive from the east coast to the west coast of Vancouver Island.

As soon as you exit from Highway 19, the pace of the drive changes. From a divided, four-lane highway, the road narrows and the speed limit drops. The trees edge closer to the road as it winds and climbs its way over the Port Alberni Summit (known by locals as "the hump") before coasting down into Port Alberni. Ascend again, this time over Mount Klitsa, and by the time the road levels out after the descent, the ocean is nearly in sight.

There's no need to hurry and no shortage of places to stop. Take a small detour to Englishman River Falls Park, where you can hike along the end of a canyon to two stunning waterfalls. After you've whetted your appetite hiking, continue to Coombs, where you can stop at the famous Old Country Market and feed yourself as you visit the goats on the roof.

From Coombs, you'll drive past Cameron Lake, where Little Qualicum Falls tumbles into a canyon near the eastern shore of the lake. Farther along, the centuries-old canopy of Cathedral Grove, a small reserve of ancient rainforest, envelops the

highway. Short paths on either side of the road lead you through the stand of old-growth forest. Try wrapping your arms around an 800-year-old tree as you wander through the trails.

Port Alberni marks the entry to the Pacific Rim as the long arm of the Alberni Inlet splashes salt water downtown. Highway 4 skirts most of the town as it descends from the Summit, but take a short trip in and around Port Alberni to pick up some snacks, or visit the historic McLean Mill a few minutes north.

From Port Alberni, kayakers heading for the Broken Group Islands can catch a ferry that operates year-round between Port Alberni and Bamfield, but for those driving all the way across Vancouver Island, the road continues. Sproat and Kennedy Lakes are two of the last freshwater attractions before Highway 4 splits at the junction between Tofino and Ucluelet.

top The Pacific Rim starts at Port Alberni, located at the end of a long saltwater inlet that flows in from the Pacific Ocean. The lighthouse by the marina is now home to the Maritime Discovery Centre.

opposite Cathedral Grove, a remnant of the ancient rainforest that once covered most of Vancouver Island, can be experienced by walking among the towering giant Douglas-firs, cedars, hemlocks and spruce trees. Some of the trees lining the pathways are more than 800 years old.

Just before arriving at the Pacific Ocean, the twisting, narrow road opens up to a spectacular view of Kennedy Lake.

top The MV *Frances Barkley* carries passengers and freight year-round to Bamfield. During the summer months, tourists can enjoy a unique alternative route to Ucluelet. The ship sails down the Port Alberni Inlet into Barkley Sound, dropping off kayakers going to the Broken Group Islands, and then continues on to either Ucluelet or Bamfield.

left Englishman River Falls plunges deep down a narrow rock canyon. Amazing views can be had from the trails along the cliff's edge.

right Larry Lake reflects the landscape like a mirror. Located next to the road, the lake makes for a perfect resting place before descending the steep, narrow road to Kennedy Lake.

opposite Spring meltwater swells the Kennedy River, which pours into and out of Kennedy Lake, the largest body of fresh water on Vancouver Island, on its journey to Tofino Inlet.

top Kennedy Lake at sunset is an outstanding place for an end-of-day picnic before heading back to Pacific Rim to spend the night.

right The drive to Pacific Rim is an awe-inspiring one, with outstanding mountain scenery and exceptional views. There is always a good chance of spotting wildlife—elk, eagles, bears or deer—while passing through this mostly uninhabited area. Evidence of the logging industry can also be seen in the form of clear-cut sections and replanted forests of young trees. This is a typical view seen from Highway 4, which crosses Vancouver Island en route to the coast.

UCLUELET

opposite The Amphitrite Point lighthouse marks the entrance to Barkley Sound and Ucluelet's harbour.

top A year-round destination, the eight-kilometre Wild Pacific Trail in Ucluelet offers spectacular viewpoints for storm-watching in winter and whale-watching in spring and summer.

Once you hit the Highway 4 junction, you have two choices: left to Ucluelet or right to Tofino. It wasn't until the highway between Ucluelet and Port Alberni was completed in 1959 that travellers to Ucluelet even had to make this choice.

Ucluelet is about eight kilometres from the pivotal Highway 4 junction, and although traditionally a centre for logging and fishing, Ucluelet has become a must-see destination in its own right.

Meaning "safe harbour" in Nuu-chah-nulth, Ucluelet has a rich history. Archaeological evidence shows that Native peoples inhabited the area for as long as 4,300 years before Europeans arrived and started establishing fur-trading, fishing and logging industries around Ucluelet in the late 19th century.

Renowned as a surf destination, Ucluelet also boasts the Wild Pacific Trail, an eight-kilometre trek that traverses the Ucluelet peninsula. Designed for walkers of all ages and abilities, the Wild Pacific Trail is planned to stretch as long as 14 kilometres when it is finally complete. With stunning views in all directions, the trail is a great spot for storm-watching in winter and whale-watching in the summer. Other wildlife may peer at you from the trees as you stroll along the gravel path.

Beachcombing, hiking, kayaking, biking, fishing, camping and picnicking are all great options for those who are less aquatically inclined than the many surfers seeking an alternative to Tofino. A quick drive from many of the great trails in the Pacific Rim National Park Reserve, Ucluelet is a great place for home base as you explore the Pacific Rim region.

Storm-watching has become one of the main activities in winter for tourists seeking a thrill. Ferocious winds and high waves pound the shore. Some brave souls might be tempted to take a chartered boat tour of the stormy seas, while others might prefer to watch the fury while cozily ensconced in a warm bed-and-breakfast. Once the tempest has passed, the beaches are littered with treasures in the form of massive logs, weathered driftwood, seaweed, fairy glass and sometimes whole trees or Japanese glass fishing floats. ᕤ

top The Wild Pacific Trail in Ucluelet has many stunning views of Barkley Sound, including this one, near the Amphitrite lighthouse.

opposite Fishing boats in the boat basin in Ucluelet near the entrance to Barkley Sound and the Broken Group Islands. Commercial and sport fishing are major industries here, thanks to the abundant fish.

top The *Canadian Princess*—permanently moored in Ucluelet—and its neighbouring hotel form the Canadian Princess Resort, an upscale fishing lodge where guests rarely go home empty-handed.

left A colourful front yard in Ucluelet, with a boat, old machinery and golden flowers.

opposite Totem poles greet visitors to the west coast. The one on the left was carved in 1972 by Charlie Mickey and the one on the right by Clifford George. Both men are from the Nuu-chah-nulth First Nations.

Waves crashing near the Wild Pacific Trail in Ucluelet. The trail meanders through old-growth forest, following the rocky headlands of the Pacific Coast. Lighthouse fans will appreciate the trail's proximity to Amphitrite Point lighthouse, a squat, unmanned lighthouse near a wicked-looking set of rocks.

top Tofino is the beginning or ending point of the Trans-Canada Highway. Once mainly a fishing village, Tofino has evolved into a resort region open all year-round.

left Float planes in Tofino. Local operators offer scenic sightseeing flights around the area, as well as service to many appealing destinations otherwise accessible only by boat.

TOFINO

If you turn right and continue along Highway 4, within another 33 kilometres you'll have reached Tofino and the end of the road—there's a sign on the First Street dock that marks the official western terminus of the Trans-Canada Highway.

On the tip of the Esowista peninsula, Tofino is bordered on three sides by ocean and the national park to the south, giving the town little room to expand in any direction. The geographic boundaries of Tofino ensure that it will never become a sprawling tourist trap of hotels, chalets, cabins and RV parks, like so many other highly sought destinations.

Like Ucluelet, Tofino had been settled for millennia by First Nations prior to European explorers. The town itself wasn't officially named until 1909, when the post office opened, even though settlers had been there since the late 1800s. The town takes its name from Tofino Inlet, which Spanish explorers Galiano and Valdés named after Vincente Tofiño (a hydrographer who taught Galiano cartography) in 1792.

With a full-time population of around 1,800 residents, Tofino sees its population increase many times over at the height of tourist season. People come to Tofino to surf, camp, play, hike, fish, relax and explore. Most people drive to the coast, but Tofino does have an airport, constructed during the Second World War, which has

three runways. The float-plane docks also make it possible to arrive in downtown Tofino by air. While the drive can take up to five hours from Victoria, a flight from Vancouver takes only an hour and provides an aerial view of the many amazing sights and scenes of the region.

Known as a surf destination since the 1960s, Tofino has a hippie vibe that permeates many of the shops and cafés. But upscale tourism has also hit the Esowista peninsula, with five-star resorts that charge hundreds of dollars per night and feature boutique spas and fine dining. Despite the multi-million-dollar resorts perched on the edge of town, Tofino hasn't lost its free-spirited soul that keeps people coming back season after season to taste, explore and revel in everything the West Coast has to offer packed into one small region. ◡

top Fishing boats sit ready for action in Tofino Inlet at the Fourth Street dock. Tofino has traditionally been a fishing village, as the area has plenty of salmon and other fish. Today visitors still delight in the abundant, sizable and delicious fish that can be caught here.

top A lone boat returning to Tofino passes Government Wharf as sunset colours the tranquil water.

right Tofino is a prime location for sea kayaking, since it has magnificent Clayoquot Sound, a UNESCO Biosphere Reserve, for its backyard. Novice paddlers can enjoy the waters of Tofino Inlet on a guided day trip with a local outfitter, while more experienced kayakers can take longer camping trips into the unspoiled heart of the Sound.

EAGLE AERIE GALLERY

ARTIST
ROY HENRY VICKERS

top The Eagle Aerie Gallery in Tofino, with its cedar plank exterior, is built like a traditional Northwest Coast longhouse. The building houses the original works of Roy Henry Vickers, a renowned artist of First Nations ancestry, who also built much of the structure using Native techniques. Vickers' colourful limited-edition prints are infused with the spirit and traditional imagery of the West Coast and its people.

left St. Columba Church in Tofino was built in 1913 to serve the growing population of this remote area. The site chosen was considered "the most beautiful spot on Vancouver Island"—and modern-day visitors still agree that it's an extremely pretty place of worship.

top Fishing boats at the Fourth Street dock. Across Tofino Inlet, the dock on Neilson Island is visible, glowing against a mountain on Meares Island beyond.

right An old boat makes a fine background for a house number in Tofino. The village is home to artists working in many media—including their yards and gardens.

top Sunset in Pacific Rim is an experience not to be missed. Frank Island, a 25-acre, privately owned island, is only a short walk to Chesterman Beach along a causeway accessible at low tide.

left A whale-watching tour sets out from Tofino in search of gray whales. Seeing a whale is a highlight of a visit to Pacific Rim for many people.

top   Visitors walk along the causeway between Chesterman Beach and Frank Island.

right   Even with the tide out (top), the rocky shore looks dangerous . . . but beautiful.

opposite   At low tide at Rosie Bay, one can explore several hidden caves and crevices that have been formed by the constant pounding of the surf.

top   Rising mist accompanies walkers enjoying Rosie Bay's beach, which is exposed only at low tide. The best time to enjoy the solitude of the empty beach is in the morning.

right   Low tide at Cox Bay at sunset exposes peaceful-looking tide pools among the rocks. However, in each small pool, some small sea creature is probably battling for its life against a hungry predator.

top Once nearly hunted to extinction for its fur, the delightful sea otter has been reintroduced along the Pacific Rim coastline.

left Bear-viewing by boat during low tide is becoming almost as popular as whale-watching. One can safely observe the bears from the water as they roll over rocks on the shoreline foraging for crabs.

PACIFIC RIM NATIONAL PARK RESERVE

The Pacific Rim National Park Reserve was established in 1970 and renegotiated in 1987. Due to ongoing treaty negotiations with the Nuu-chah-nulth, Pacific Rim is considered a national park reserve, which means that Parks Canada acknowledges there may be outstanding rights or claims to the land.

While negotiations are ongoing, the region is managed and protected like all national parks. Comprised of three units, Long Beach, the West Coast Trail and the Broken Group Islands, Pacific Rim National Park Reserve protects more than 500 square kilometres.

Long Beach

Perhaps the best-known part of the Pacific Rim (and definitely the most accessible part), Long Beach stretches for nearly 20 kilometres along Wickaninnish Bay between Tofino and Ucluelet. Long Beach is home to the Kʷisitis Visitor Centre (formerly known as the Wickaninnish Interpretive Centre) and the Green Point Campground, both open seasonally. Home to the best surfing in Canada, Long Beach is filled nearly to capacity on hot summer days, but the local surfers hit the waves year-round, carving the waves on all but the harshest winter days.

Broken Group Islands

Accessible only by boat, the Broken Group Islands comprise more than 100 islands and islets in Barkley Sound. Renowned as a place for great kayaking and boating, the islands are ideal for an aquatic camping trip. Blessed with sheltered waters, the Broken Group Islands offer the quintessential West Coast experience—big trees, open ocean, wildlife and mountain views—without some of the usual hazards found in other popular Vancouver Island boating destinations, namely rough seas, exposed passages and high winds.

West Coast Trail

Built in the early 1900s as a life-saving trail, the West Coast Trail is a 75-kilometre trek from Bamfield to Port Renfrew. Although it had fallen into disuse by the 1950s, the West Coast Trail was reopened in 1973. It is now one of the most popular and most challenging multi-day hikes in North America. People often take five to seven days to complete the full trek, covering a broad range of terrain: ancient forests, sandy beaches, rocky paths, mud and everything in between. And the weather is as changeable as the terrain.

top   The Broken Group Islands consist of more than 100 forested islands, islets and rocky outcrops. The calm waters of the inner islands of Barkley Sound are perfect for kayaking and boating.

opposite   Seagulls in front of a wind-tossed sea at Combers Beach.

top Silhouetted surfers head out into a perfect swell. Surfing is possible year-round on the west coast of Vancouver Island, but it's most popular in summer, when the water is warmer.

left Paddle surfing (or surf kayaking) is another way to enjoy the wild waves that roll in from the Pacific.

top The ocean's in motion as waves crash against the rocks at Schooner Cove, which is at the very north end of Long Beach, just inside the national park boundary.

right A giant green anemone and purple sea urchins share a tide pool.

This is truly the western edge of Canada. The Pacific Ocean surf rolls in unbroken for hundreds of kilometres before hitting the sand of Wickaninnish Beach, sometimes bringing huge drift logs with it.

top Even at the height of summer, the waters of the Pacific are chilly. However, on a hot, sunny day, hardy swimmers take to the waves just off Green Point Campground on Long Beach.

left The lush and constantly expanding forest comes right to the edge of the pavement on most roads in the area. Pictured here is the tranquil road leading to the Kʷisitis Visitor Centre.

top, right The Rainforest Trail in Pacific Rim offers a quiet boardwalk stroll through an ancient old-growth forest. Interpretive plaques tell the story of the forest's life cycle. The trees—some of which are many centuries old—are truly magnificent, reaching incredible sizes thanks to the plentiful rainfall here: over 300 centimetres per year. When they eventually topple, the fallen logs become home to new shoots of trees that will, in their turn, become giants.

The Rainforest Trail abounds with flora and fauna. Pacific Rim is home to black-tailed deer (inset top) and black bears (inset bottom), as well as many other life forms, such as moss and fungi, which make their home in the trees (inset middle).

top A stroll along Combers Beach on a calm autumn afternoon will offer plenty of solitude and scenery. The forces of tide and erosion are dramatically evident here along the beach, which has an ever-shifting shoreline. Take the Spruce Fringe trail from this parking lot to learn more about the effects of the sea and wind on the forest bordering the beach.

left Long Beach logs can provide makeshift shelters . . . or impromptu art. As far up the beach as these logs are, they are nonetheless covered by high tides about 10 percent of the time.

top The view out to sea from Wickaninnish Beach is of pounding surf. The KʷISitis Visitor Centre is perched above this stretch of sand. The handsomely weathered wooden building is a must-see for most visitors, who come to learn about the natural and human history of this windswept part of the world. The effects of the Pacific Ocean are explored through displays, films, special events and activities for children and adults.

right Seagulls gather at low tide to see what the ocean has left for them to eat on Combers Beach. The beach is a great place for birdwatching and spotting sea lions.

top The Kʷisitis Visitor Centre catches the last rays of the day. The restaurant here, with its huge windows facing the water, offers superb dining and one of the best sunset viewpoints in the area.

left Waves crashing onto the rocks near the Kʷisitis Visitor Centre. Wickaninnish was a powerful and wealthy local chief during the peak of the sea otter trade in the late 18th century. His name has been given to numerous places in the area.

top Wickaninnish Beach is a wonderful place for a stroll. The parking lot at the Visitor Centre is a trailhead for several short walks, including a sometimes muddy—but always interesting—2.5-kilometre walk over old corduroy roads and cedar boardwalks through the forest to Florencia Bay.

right Frothing surf at Lismer Beach. Even in sheltered coves such as this, the waters of the Pacific can be powerful, and swimming is not recommended.

top Gazing at Wya Point at Florencia Bay under a tranquil moon, it's hard to imagine this could be a treacherous site for ships. However, the area was formerly known as Wreck Bay, after a ship named *Florencia* foundered here in 1861. The beach here is wide and open, perfect for strolling, sunbathing or even wading in the surf.

left Florencia Bay and neighbouring Halfmoon Bay are tucked away at the southern tip of the Long Beach Unit of Pacific Rim National Park Reserve, not far from Ucluelet. Here, smooth beach stones offer a perfect place for a romantic sunset walk.

opposite Looking into the early rays of sunset off Long Beach, it seems as if the ocean stretches endlessly and, for the moment, peacefully.

CLAYOQUOT SOUND

opposite The oldest living cedar tree in Clayoquot Sound is on Meares Island.

top The orca, or killer whale, is actually the largest of the dolphins and shares that species' agility and grace.

If you keep heading north once you get to Tofino, you'll end up right in the waters of Clayoquot Sound. Many of the waters surrounding the Pacific Rim are part of Clayoquot Sound, a vast network of inlets, islands and sounds. Some of the bigger islands are Flores, Vargas and Meares. Archaeological evidence shows that several of the islands in Clayoquot Sound have been inhabited continuously by First Nations for 5,000 years. The major inlets of Clayoquot Sound include Shelter, Herbert, Tofino, Bedwell and Lemmens.

Rich in culture, natural beauty, wildlife and landscape, Clayoquot Sound has been at the forefront of some of the biggest environmental battles in Canada. Logging of the old-growth forest is still a contentious issue. Protests against a decision to allow nearly two-thirds of the ancient timber to be cut in 1993 brought huge amounts of international attention to the region, and the debate continues today. While the protests in the early '90s were ultimately successful, the ancient rainforests of Clayoquot Sound are still at risk.

Residents and visitors to the Pacific Rim are constantly awed by the beauty and diversity of the region. In 2000, UNESCO designated Clayoquot Sound a biosphere reserve, recognizing the importance of environmental, economic and social

sustainability. The designation came with a $12-million endowment to be used for research, conservation and education.

Millions of whales migrate through Clayoquot Sound each spring, making whale-watching a popular adventure. Many companies charter tours, but you can also catch glimpses from the beaches or the many hiking paths around Clayoquot Sound. Clayoquot Sound is also home to many endangered species of birds and animals, making it a naturalist's hot spot.

Kayaking, hiking and camping are all popular activities around Clayoquot Sound. Many islands have developed camping and hiking spots, and there are always plans under way to expand and improve the current network of trails.

top Steller sea lions are frequently seen in Pacific Rim and Clayoquot Sound, where they dine on salmon and other fish. A full-grown male can weigh up to 380 kilograms and can swim at up to 40 kilometres per hour. If you do encounter one, keep your distance. They are wild animals, despite their fun-loving nature.

opposite Every spring, residents of Pacific Rim rejoice in the return of gray whales from their winter breeding grounds off the coast of Baja California. Once nearly hunted to extinction, the gray whale—now plenti-ful—is a symbol of hope for many.

top   View from Tofino toward the village of Opitsat on Meares Island, which is home to the Tla-o-qui-aht (pronounced Ta-LOW-kwee-at) Band. The island is covered by a magnificent old-growth forest, including the Hanging Garden Cedar, which is over 2,000 years old and 18 metres in circumference.

left   The protected waters of Browning Passage near Tofino attract many tourists new to the popular sport of kayaking.

opposite   A two-kilometre boardwalk carved with the names of many sailing vessels leads you through an old-growth forest ending at the Hot Springs Cove waterfall by the ocean.

top First Nations cedar canoes in Clayoquot Sound. These canoes were traditionally roughed out in the forest, then finished in the village. They ranged in size from 3 to 15 metres long. Whaling canoes were between 9 and 11 metres long—some 3 to 5 metres shorter than the gray whales the Nuu-chah-nulth hunted with harpoons.

left Ahousaht chiefs and their crews complete a canoe quest in traditional hand-carved cedar canoes.

opposite A Native woman is resplendent in a traditional West Coast First Nations button blanket and cedar hat as she beats her drum on the beach at an Ahousaht canoe gathering.

Ahousat Harbour, Flores Island. Many visitors come here on day trips to hike the 16-kilometre Wild Side Heritage Trail that connects the village with the island's many secluded beaches. Inset: Detail of the eagle head on a Nuu-chah-nulth cedar canoe (top); the images on a handmade whaler's cedar-bark hat celebrate the whale hunt (middle); salmon roasting on an open cedar fire (bottom).

Orca in
Clayoquot Sound.

Ole Hoyer and Wendy Snowdon graduated from Ryerson University in photographic arts. Their work has been published worldwide in numerous magazines, calendars and books. While travelling and freelancing in Europe, Ole and Wendy produced images for more than 25 books on that continent's countries and regions. They live in North Vancouver, BC.